The Ultimate Guide To:

<u>Talk To Anyone!</u>

Use Charisma And Self Confidence To Talk To People And Get Anything You Want!

Ryan Cooper

STOP!!! Before you read any further....Would you like to know the Secrets of Transforming your life, overcome insecurities, develop leadership skills, and undeniable confidence in your personal, professional, and relationship life?

If your answer is yes, then you are not alone. Thousands of people are looking for the secret to have unstoppable confidence and self-driven power in all areas of their lives.

If you have been searching for these answers without much luck, you're in the right place!

Not only will you gain incredible insight in this book, but because I want to make sure to give you as much value as possible, right now for a limited time you can get full **100% FREE access to a VIP bonus EBook** entitled **LIMITLESS ENERGY!**

Just Go Here For Free Instant Access:

www.PotentialRise.com

Legal Notice

Disclaimer Notice

information contained herein on the new conditions whenever they see applicable.

Table Of Contents

Introduction

I want to thank you and congratulate you for purchasing the book, *"Talk To Anyone: The Ultimate Guide To Talk To Anyone! - Use Charisma And Self Confidence To Talk To People And Get Anything You Want!"*.

Talk To Anyone And Get What You Want!

This book contains proven steps and strategies on how to easily persuade people and get what you want!

Most people don't realize the incredible power we have in our words, if we just open our mouth in front of the right people we will undoubtedly get what we want, if we say it with the proper delivery and self confidence!

Charisma is a learned skill and anyone can be self confident and influence people if you know the proper steps and strategies outlined in this book.

At the same time, this book will show you how you can be impressive and charming just by being yourself. Yes, you are bound to be liked by the people you encounter everyday for being who you are. Everyone is free to attract the people that they need in their life, and that means that you can continuously grow your network and fill it with relevant people, as long as you know how to develop yourself. This book will show you how to do that. You will also learn the secrets of making the perfect first impressions, and getting the most out of the most ordinary conversations.

Thanks again for purchasing this book, I hope you enjoy it!

Chapter 1 – Are you Really Shy?

A lot of people struggle with shyness, but what is this trait really? Shyness, which is also called diffidence, is characterized as that feeling of being awkward, unconfident or apprehensive when there are other people, particularly strangers, around. For most people, shyness is more often experienced by people who have low self-esteem. When this trait is taken to another level, people tend to develop social phobia or social anxiety.

Is it Normal to be Shy?

Shyness is actually a developed trait, which means that it is triggered by a number of events that led a person to acquire it later on in life. It is, after all, an ego-driven trait that makes people concerned about what others might be thinking about them. Most of the time, it is developed when a person feels physical anxiety towards unknown circumstances.

Some people also believe that shyness can be a genetic trait. For example, fearful children are often raised by fearful parents. At the same time, children who are raised by parents with self-esteem issues can also develop a similar behavioral pattern.

Shyness, because of the above reasons, is considered normal. Society believes that there are outgoing people, and then there are people who have difficulty expressing their concerns. There are also people who have experienced awkwardness or being laughed at, simply because they act the way they are trained to do. When you look at this condition closely and understand that being shy is due to the fact that some people are made to believe that they should be uncomfortable with the way they look or act, shyness can be overcome.

Do You Believe You Are Shy?

If you think that you are shy, you have a reason to believe that it is true. After all, everything that you say about yourself is what your mind will perceive about yourself. Most of the time, what you say about yourself is a self-fulfilling prophecy – say something about yourself, even if it does not really make sense, and then eventually it would become true.

If you observe how bullies can manage to destroy a person's self-esteem, they call their victims names, which in turn, defines them. However, it does not mean that what they are saying is true. They just say it repeatedly, and over time, their name-calling sticks. That would be the same with the way a shy person would do to himself. For this very reason, it is very possible for a person to be his own worst enemy.

To make it simpler, you are shy because you admit to that truth, even when you know that it could possibly hurt you. You have simply taken that description for yourself and you want to believe that for a very long time. However, you do not have to believe that as long as you live, especially if it is beginning to impair your relationship with others, or the way you should have taken opportunities.

However, there is always that opportunity to believe that you are otherwise. Shyness, most of the time, is one's own perception of himself, and once that belief is changed, a once-shy person can become an empowered person. When you think about it, you can easily overturn that awkwardness and become a confident person. You can even regain your confidence in an instant, if you put in the work.

Regaining Your Confidence

Some people would consider that being self-confident is a lifetime endeavor. However, for some people, it would be the other case – all it would take them is a chance to redeem their self-belief. When you look at how some people grew up and became billionaires as adults, they did not come from backgrounds that would actually reinforce self-esteem. Some of them grew up from a poor family, some of them even came from broken homes. Some of them also had received the worst rejection letters. They were called failures, and definitely treated like misfits.

If you think that you cannot overcome the challenge of being awkward, or being that person at the party who cannot look anyone in the eye, think about this – what if you could? What if you can actually take that promotion in your office? What if you can actually be in a band and not worry about money? What if you can actually live your dreams, even if there are bullies around you who say otherwise?

If you are very concerned about what other people are thinking about you, then you should know that these people are also concerned about how they look like or if they can get the approval of others through what they do. In a nutshell, they are most probably more conscious about themselves that they would barely notice you. Pay attention to them, or give them a random compliment. You would be surprised at how they would react.

Just thinking about the amount of leverage that you can get when you are confident would definitely help you land you to places. It may be painful for you to move out of your comfort zone, but it will be worth it. All it takes is to break barriers one by one. Start a conversation with a stranger, or say hi to people at work. Doing things that you are not used to do will reveal all the other things that you can do in the near future.

Chapter 2 – The Secret To Being A Good Conversationalist

Ever wondered what every random conversation can get you? If you look back in time, random conversations might have landed you your best romantic relationship ever, or your first comfortable job. When you dig deeper into your previous conversations, you would figure out that there is a lot more that you can get out of every word that you say.

Look at the lifestyle of the best NBA players, award-winning movie stars and software moguls. It is possible that they started out as any plain Joe that you would know in your neighborhood. They have done something great during the years of practicing their careers, but there sure is something that they are still doing to keep them at the top.

It is not about the skills that they need to do their profession. But all people need to see that it is very important to talk to someone the right way in order for them to land their first job, or to get their big break. However, not everyone gets a manager to handle the conversations that would make them land their dream jobs.

More often than not, people are supposed to do their own negotiations to get what they need out of other people. Those needs range from small changes to big dream contracts. Being able to say what you have in mind would also protect you from being manipulated to do something that you do not want to do. This ability would get you covered in finding out that you need to approach what you need to get what you truly want. It is also the ability that would allow you to use your other skills for a much longer time.

The Secret Sauce to Speaking

You might have known people who talk smoothly over drinks, but you do not really need a drink in order to be able to talk well and say what you want to say. All it takes is to have the confidence to do so. You start with telling yourself every morning that you have what it takes, and that would allow you to say the right words in front of a client or an employer.

Being confident would also allow you to manage to think about all the things that you can do in the future. It is very much like what sales representatives and the most successful job applicants do. They know that they may be lacking some expertise or experience at a certain field, and they may not be too optimistic that they will land a job or a sale. However, they hold the certainty that they will be able to fill up that experience void once they have the opportunity.

Confident people are the ones who are willing to do whatever it takes to take the opportunity that they need to excel. The only reason they have is that they believe that they deserve it, and there is no one else in their mind that can make the most out of that opportunity. Because of this confidence, they are capable of working harder than those who have less self-esteem.

It is beyond your wildest imagination where confidence can take you. It is like a natural high, and it is something that would bewilder your senses and keep you saying the right words and wear the right face to work. However, confidence is not plain arrogance or bullheadedness. It is having the ability to believe in yourself that you can make it out of a difficult situation because you are clearheaded enough to think of what you should do. It is not being too optimistic. It is being able to see things as they are.

Chapter 3 – What You Get Out Of Small Talks

If you do not like small talks, then you may be that type of person who would like to have few, but meaningful conversations. It is understandable that you may not think that conversations about the weather or the game are anything of substance. You may think that small talks are bound to be meaningless and insincere. However, you may think about these small talks differently starting today – these cheap talks may actually be your ticket to better relationships and more opportunities.

Looking Deeper into Conversations

You have to admit that it will always take a while before a person can get comfortable with you. You have to have that first conversation that would propel things into motion. More likely, you have opened a small talk with most of your friends, and that made you more interesting.

Small talks usually happen spontaneously – it is not planned, and what would come out first would stem out of your personality. They give away so much of what you are interested in and how interested you really are in the person whom you are talking to. Striking these conversations also reveal if you are willing to make that extra mile to make a person feel like he is in good company, and then develop friendship with him.

These conversations are also one of the most effective ways to boost your self-esteem. A random conversation makes you feel comfortable about yourself, and it enables you to know what other people like in you. It makes you pay attention to a lot of details, making you able to live in a moment. These conversations make you feel aware about your surroundings, and it makes you put down your Smartphone to see what is happening in real life. At the same time, research says that making friendly conversations can actually make you smarter – social interactions boost your creativity and your ability to solve problems.

When you think about it, the rest of the people around you would actually pay real money to have small conversations. Mark Zuckerberg made Facebook for the sake of making people connected to each other, no matter how far they are from each other.

At the same time, making these small talks would help you create that possibility that you can invite a person out the next time you see each other, or make a very good working relationship with him. A lot of professionals make it a point that they make small talks with the people whom they want to work with in the future. That makes it possible for them to make their future relationship a lot easy to realize, and get past the usual awkwardness of starting a new relationship with a person who they look forward to having a professional relationship with. When you look at it closely, you can actually make your relationship with a future boss or a client better, before you even start working together.

Conversations will Eventually Matter

When you think about it, that first conversation that you made with someone would be that kind talk that would remind that person of you the next time you meet. You would always make good impressions that will help you get the leverage when you know what kind of small talks you should open up for starters. Small talks also show how capable you are in observing what could possibly make that other person interested in you.

The foolproof way of starting a conversation the right way is to actually do some research about the person who you want to meet. Make use of the information that you can find on social media sites to know what particular type of conversations they would find appealing, or ask your common friends about a few information about them. However, you may want to only use this information to start a relevant story to open up more topics. You definitely would not want to make them feel like they are being watched.

Making Good Impressions

When starting a small talk, do not force yourself to be someone that you are not – you will be liked by people just the way you are. Remember that if you are planning on making a long-term relationship with others, they will find out more about you in the long run. The best way to make sure that your relationship would run smoothly is to keep it real.

At the same time, be a sensible and sensitive conversationalist. Do not force conversations – this would make you sound like you are trying too hard, or you are being desperate to sell them something. Also, make sure that you also allow others to speak. Know when you should talk, and know when it's time to listen. At the same time, be sensitive enough to learn when it is okay to change topics. You can talk about something else when the conversation stalls – take it as the cue to talk about anything else that the other person might be interested in.

Being a good conversationalist would actually require you to pay more attention to the other person, rather than making them pay attention to you. Most people are more likely to build friendships when they feel that you are more interested in them, rather than making them interested in you. To keep the conversation going and to know more about that person whom you are talking to, make sure that you also ask follow up questions whenever they provide clues about themselves. When they talk about their work, ask about how long they have been in their industry, or what their expertise is.

If you think that you do not have enough confidence to talk to others, don't worry. Even the richest men and the most successful executives experience jitters when they are about to talk to someone who they do not know, especially when

they feel that that person is more important than them, or if they are hoping that they can get something fruitful out of the conversation. Nevertheless, psychiatrist Steven Berglas gave this advice for those who are struggling with their self-esteem: there are two phases when it comes to building self-confidence – you have to eliminate self-doubt, then you start to make yourself believe in the things that you have already accomplished and the other things that you can do.

Chapter 4 – Charming People To Get What You Want

Now, what can you do to make small talks work to your advantage? When you think about it, there is a certain characteristic that can turn any conversation to leverage, or allow you to convince people that you are important and that they should work with you. That trait is called charisma.

You can call a person charismatic when he can instantly make people feel important. Some can even say that a person can make the room feel livelier whenever he walks in. You can even say that he lights up the entire building whenever he smiles.

Everybody wants to be a charismatic person, simply because a person who has charm can enable people to do things that they want to do. They eliminate any kind of self-doubt. They are the most optimistic people that you will meet, and you feel that they are better than most people you know.

Positive confidence can give a special characteristic to a person that even before they speak up, you know that they are important. In addition, everybody wants to feel that. Most people are struggling with confidence that they are unsure if they can repeat anything that they were able to do successfully in the past. Some people struggle with roles that society assigned them. They find that they cannot do anything about expectations. Without that confidence, some people feel lost.

How to Turn Your Natural Charisma On

Charisma is actually all about the other person – by making the other person feel empowered, you can get him to be on your side. That is why the most charismatic people are those who are able to make others feel good about themselves, not the other way around. They use their positivity to make others make the right decisions and at the same time, they make them aware that they are able to do so with their help.

However, the most charming people use their charm in such a way that other people are aware that they do not do special favors all the time. When you think about it, turning your charm on when you need it would be better. That would make the other person think that you are giving him special attention, which you would not normally do to others. However, be careful that you do not turn out to be too revealing about your intentions – you do not want other people to think that you are just being nice because you want to get something from them.

Make the entire conversation all about them. If they begin to feel that the entire universe revolves around them, the better. That would make them immediately comfortable around you, and that would allow you to lead them to the "real" conversation that you want to talk about. As much as possible, do not let your ego drive the conversation – nobody would really want you to talk about yourself and what you want to get from them.

However, people like to listen to a person who is not presentable, or does not look confident at all. For this reason, always make sure that you look the part that oozes.

Learn How to Study Body Language

If you want others to pay extra attention to you, you also have to pay more attention to how they are behaving. You would notice that there are certain triggers that would grab other people's attention. Here's the trick – acting like how they would normally behave makes you more attractive. The only reason for that is that people normally like themselves, and they feel compelled to build a relationship with a person who is very much like them.

Body language and charisma go together well. You would notice that most people's posture stoops when they are not confident or when they are feeling bad. You would also notice that there are certain people who are more likely to pay attention to you if you use certain words that appeal to the senses that they use the most.

For example, you would most likely get a person who is musically inclined to buy headphones from you if you describe more about the quality of sound. However, visual people would likely pay more attention on how it looks like.

Remember that certain words have different impact on different people, and a charismatic person is very careful about the words that they use. If your charm is turned "on," you have to make sure that you use words that are more compelling or empowering. You may choose to use words that encourage immediate action, or you may also use words that would suggest that the other person has the time to decide. However, if you are trying to get them to agree, do not suggest that they have the option to say no. You can imply instead that they are going to make a decision favorable to you sooner or later.

Following that same logic, you can use adverbs like looks, sounds, seems, smells, or tastes, before any adjective to make a better appeal. You can also try mirroring the other person's posture so that you can level better with him. That would make the other person feel that you are trying to establish friendship with him. Remember, you should only mirror his actions, but you should not mimic him.

Other Things to Keep in Mind

Charming people know how to tell great stories, and they have great sense of humor. They are also the type of people who use words with certainty, and they always have conviction. They are also the type of people who would want their names to be remembered. When they introduce themselves, they make sure that the other person hears their name clearly. They even make it a point to say their names or their point twice.

What makes them extra attractive to a lot of people is that they are the most emphatic people that you would know. They are good listeners, and they have keen attention to details. For that reason, they become excellent problem-solvers, because they make it a point to have wide network and resources. They are also among the most humble people that you would ever know in your circle because they are not the type who'd brag about their achievements. They are also the type of people who would not say bad things about others. These are the reasons why charismatic people are capable of getting the best network in every industry that they are in.

Getting these characteristics are easy – you just have to make sure that you are confident, have a good grasp of reality, and you are capable of giving more attention to others. Having these traits would allow you to have that charm that you have always wanted.

Chapter 5 – Making Great Use Of Your Network

Confidence and having a great attitude towards others is your ticket to having the best things in life. This combination is what you are going to need when you plan to get more opportunities. This combination will help you become successful, or even become one of the top 1%.

Speaking of the one percent, you are not likely to get to the top if you are not aware of how to make the right friends. Connections are very important in such a way that they allow you to tap more opportunities than you can get on your own. For that reason, billionaires, entrepreneurs, and salespersons always aim to surround themselves with people who would make positive impact on their careers. You should also do the same starting today.

You do not really have much choice other than being connected to other people, unless you plan on living a solitary life. You need these connections to land good deals, and you need your network to get news that is relevant to your career. That is why it is very important for people to think about what kind of friends they should make.

How to Attract the Right Kind of People

Have you ever heard about the Law of Attraction? This philosophy adheres to the belief that a person can only attract the things that he has asked for. That means that the friends and acquaintances that you make may have been a surprise, but there is something in your aura that attracted those kinds of people. In such a way, you have chosen them to become part of your life.

However, there are people who believe that they might have been successful if not for their friends. They think that the wrong company is the reason for their financial or social problems.

Nevertheless, you can easily see that they have been attracting those people because of their lifestyle.

People are always bound to attract people who are very much like them, just like you are more likely to establish friendship with someone who is like you. That is human nature. People would only want those who embody their beliefs and values, and that is normal. Therefore, if you would tend to complain about the type of people that you have in your life, think that they are the reflection of your value system. You would definitely have to change your values if you want to improve the type of people who tend to hold on to you. To make it simple, improving yourself will also improve the type of people you attract.

Keep Growing Your Network

You will never know what would happen to your life later on. As your needs become more complex, you notice that you need more people in your life. You may even change careers, or get in a mix that you would need a hand out. For that reason, you need to meet as many people as you can, and establish good relationships with them.

With this in mind, how can you keep growing your network? There are plenty of ways to do so. Nowadays, you can make use of the Internet to keep track of the people you know, and to make sure that they will always hear from you. You can add your contacts to your Facebook network, or if you want to have a separate Internet circle for your professional contacts, then you can use LinkedIn to connect with them. That would enable you to separate professional discussions from the ones that you make with your peers.

You would also want to make blogs and follow others that have similar interests with yours. This will allow you to make use of your blogs to connect with people overseas, or to discover people who work in niches that would be relevant to the opportunities that you want to tap. Later on, you would want to reach out to them and add them as your personal or professional contact.

At the same time, make yourself very accessible in life outside the Internet as well. Make sure that your existing contacts invite you to events. See to it that you return the favor as well, so that they will keep introducing you to the people that you definitely like to meet.

How to Make New People Want to Be Your Contact

There are several occasions wherein you will probably experience that awkward feeling of being dismissed, as if the new people you just met wouldn't want to do anything with you in the future. There are possible scenarios on why this would happen: you might have come out as too strong for them, or they might have felt that you are just trying to establish a relationship that will be just about your needs.

The key to making new contacts, especially if you really want them, is to make other people feel like they will need you in the future. In a nutshell, you would want to make them feel that you have something to offer them. You should remember that other people are bound to feel that they should honor favors by returning them, because they would feel that you are a valuable contact.

When you meet new people, it is very important to make them feel that you have something important in common. Try to find a connection immediately once you are introduced to each other, and you can do that by listening well to their introduction about themselves and by adding follow up questions afterwards. When you introduce yourself, make sure that you use a unique description of yourself, but keep it short. At this point, nobody would really want to listen to your accomplishments.

Make sure that you also carry a business card with you to make sure that the new contacts you make will know how to reach you. However, be sensitive on the timing on when you should give them to others. It is customary to wait for the other person to ask for your card, before you give it to him. It is also best to give your business card just before you end your conversation. It would be best to do if you know that your initial talk really went well. It is a guarantee that you would hear soon from that person.

Listen well to what the other person says during the initial conversation. You will find out that they would be mentioning some ideas or problems in mind, and scan your memory for any contact in your network that might be able to help them. That does a favor to your existing contact, and that would make that new person recognize you as a person in the industry to be reckoned with.

Keeping it Real

When trying to grow and maintain your network, it is very important to be impressive, but still, you have to be yourself. Whenever you talk to a new person, make sure that you are tapping your best assets, but never lie about the things that you can do. That would enable you to be liked for who you really are.

Conclusion

Thank you again for purchasing this book on talking to anyone and getting whatever you want!

I am extremely excited to pass this information along to you, and I am so happy that you now have read and can hopefully implement these strategies going forward.

I hope this book was able to help you understand more about the power of communication and how it can help you to accomplish your goals.

The next step is to get started using this information and begin living a much more fulfilling life!

If you know of anyone else that could benefit from the information presented here please inform them of this book.

Finally, if you enjoyed this book and feel it has added value to your life in any way, please take the time to share your thoughts and post a review on Amazon. It'd be greatly appreciated!

Thank you and good luck!

Preview Of:

The Ultimate Guide To:

<u>Small Talk!</u>

Quickly Overcome Shyness And Social Anxiety, And Talk To Anyone With These Proven Communication Skills!

Introduction

I want to thank you and congratulate you for purchasing the book, *"Small Talk: The Ultimate Guide To Small Talk! - Quickly Overcome Shyness And Social Anxiety, And Talk To Anyone With These Proven Communication Skills!"*

This book on "Small Talk" contains proven steps and strategies on how to overcome shyness, social anxiety, or even moderate discomfort when speaking to strangers!

You will never know how greatly someone can benefit your life or how you can benefit theirs in some way if you don't speak to them! You might meet a special someone....Or just imagine the new friends you could have if you just simply talk to people when you are in public! Also, consider the advantages that you would have professionally if you weren't afraid to spark up a conversation with strangers.

If you have ever felt shy about talking to other people or even just being in other people's presence, then you are not alone. Many people feel uncomfortable with having to strike up conversations, especially if they have to do so with strangers. There are those who would prefer to keep to themselves and even those who would consciously try to avoid being with others as much as possible.

However, being human is as much about being social beings as it is about breathing, eating and sleeping. That is, for one reason or another, you will have to face other people, mingle with them and participate in conversations properly.

Thanks again for purchasing this book, I hope you enjoy it!

Chapter 1: Shyness And How To Overcome It

Shyness is not something to be ashamed of. As funny as that may sound, everyone undergoes this feeling of shyness in one way or another. Do you remember the time when you had to stand in front of the whole class to introduce yourself? Or that time when you had to be in front of your boss and other business partners so that you could deliver your report? How about that moment when you had to give a speech on your best friend's wedding or on your parents' anniversary?

Even when you just meet people for the first time, it is not uncommon to have a feeling of uneasiness that keeps you from saying the right things or that keeps you wanting to run away as fast and as far as possible. You feel nervous and anxious, and all you could do is wish that you had never been in that situation in the first place.

Many people have the misconception that only introverted people experience shyness. Introverts, after all, are known for avoiding social situations because they often prefer to be with themselves rather than with other people, but it is very different from having the feeling of shyness. On the contrary, shyness is that tendency to feel tense or awkward and sometimes even worried during social encounters. Most of the time, this feeling of unease is associated with social interactions with strangers, but it can also happen in different situations.

It is said that shyness can be observed through certain symptoms. Some people who are shy can easily blush when faced with an awkward moment. For others, shyness brings with it sweating, the quick pounding of the heart and even the feeling of an upset stomach. There are also times when shyness sets off less physical manifestations such as that of the person who is shy as having negative feelings about themselves. People who are shy tend to worry about how other people will look at them or how other people see them, and thus they would rather withdraw from social interactions than to have to worry about other people's perception of them.

Following these facts, it is not easy to find that everyone undergoes shyness at least at one point in their lives. Even the most confident person can feel shy about meeting the person of his or her dreams, and even more so towards meeting that person's parents and other family members. A well-established businessman would also feel anxious when it comes to dealing with new partners or perhaps when it comes to addressing the shareholders, despite the fact that he or she is already very much respected and looked up upon. And even the world's greatest leaders would probably stumble and falter when given unexpected praises or comments.

Again, there is nothing to be ashamed of when it comes to being shy. It comes naturally just as much as breathing is naturally a part of being alive. However, if you find yourself feeling shy and you know that the shyness is keeping you from doing what you must, then there is something that has to be done. The good thing is, there are more ways of overcoming shyness than you may think.

Feelings of shyness often come from being too self-conscious or from being overly worried about what other people may think. In some cases, this can lead to awkward social moments where the shy person stutters or finds it hard to maintain eye contact or any level of physical contact, but in other worst cases, it can also lead to intense social phobia. The most common occurrences of shyness are associated with interactions with authority figures such as teachers, bosses, and leaders, with romantic interests and also with various group settings.

Overcoming Shyness

Those who wish to overcome their shyness should put utmost importance into understanding what their shyness is all about. Take note that this is not just about understanding what shyness is, but more about having a clearer idea about what their personal shyness truly is.

Each person experiences shyness in a unique way. The cause for shyness varies, the signs and symptoms also differ, but most importantly, the source or the reason for shyness is also different from one person to another. Before you can go on trying to overcome your shyness, you should have a deeper understanding of what it is all about and where it stems from. By knowing the source, you have a much better chance of addressing the issue from its root and therefore get more favorable results from overcoming shyness.

There are three main reasons why people tend to feel shyness. The first of these is a weak self-image. When you see yourself as someone who is never enough or someone who always does the wrong things, chances are that you will always be anxious around other people. Unfortunately, how you think about yourself or what you see yourself doing is often manifested into the real world. This means that if you believe that you will do something wrong, you most probably will.

However, this also means that the solution is very simple – stop thinking so negatively about yourself! This is easier said than done, but it is one of the most fundamental ways of how you can overcome shyness. Remember that a weak self-image is just a voice inside your head. But that voice is your mind and what you are thinking. Tell that voice to shut up or better yet, make that voice say the opposite of the negative things that you are thinking.

The second main reason why people tend to feel shy is because they are too conscious of how they may come off to other people. It may only be natural for human beings to be conscious of what other people may be thinking about them, but to be unable to function properly as a result of this is never a good thing. Those who are shy because of this reason will spend hours and hours preparing themselves so that they look good in front of other people.

Even so, they will always be conscious about every move they make and whether or not they are turning other people off. The simple solution to this is to not focus on one's self too much. Other people are probably thinking of other things besides you anyway, so you should do the same thing.

Finally, people also tend to become shy because other people actually think that they are shy. When you are labeled as being shy, there is a greater tendency to actually experience shyness in social situations. Even if that person being labeled as shy is willing to overcome the label, the problem is that those who have labeled them will still treat them as such. Then again, this is all just a matter of perception. So what if other people think that you are shy? The more that others think this way, the greater the reason you have for proving them otherwise.

All of these reasons have their own validity, but the simple fact is that you have to get over these thoughts if you want to overcome shyness. Stop thinking negatively about yourself, do not stress yourself too much about what other people may think and actually get over what other people think of you. Overcoming shyness starts with accepting that you are shy, understanding why that is so, and having a conscious effort of turning things around.

Thanks for Previewing My Exciting Book Entitled:

"Small Talk: Quickly Overcome Shyness And Social Anxiety, And Talk To Anyone With These Proven Communication Skills!"

To purchase this book, simply go to the Amazon Kindle store and simply search:

"SMALL TALK"

Then just scroll down until you see my book. You will know it is mine because you will see my name "Ryan Cooper" underneath the title.

Alternatively, you can visit my author page on Amazon to see this book and other work I have done. Thanks so much, and please don't forget your free bonuses

DON'T LEAVE YET! - CHECK OUT YOUR FREE BONUSES BELOW!

Free Bonus Offer: Get Free Access To The PotentialRise.com VIP Newsletter!

Once you enter your email address you will immediately get free access to this awesome newsletter!

But wait, right now if you join now for free you will also get free access to the "LIMITLESS ENERGY" free EBook!

To claim both your FREE VIP NEWSLETTER MEMBERSHIP and your FREE BONUS Ebook on LIMITLESS ENERGY!

Just Go To:

www.PotentialRise.com

www.ingramcontent.com/pod-product-compliance
Lightning Source LLC
Chambersburg PA
CBHW071559170526
45166CB00004B/1718